The Nature Kid's Guide to
PUFFINS

DAVID ANDERSON

LP Media Inc. Publishing
Text copyright © 2026 by LP Media Inc.

For information address LP Media Inc. Publishing,
30012 Variolite St NW, Princeton MN 55371
www.lpmedia.org

Publication Data

Puffins
The Nature Kid's Guide to Puffins — First edition.

Summary: "Learn all about Puffins, the Nature Kid Way"
— Provided by publisher.

ISBN: 979-8-89818-199-4

[1. Puffins – Non-Fiction] I. Title.

Title: The Nature Kid's Guide to Puffins

CONTENTS

CLIFF LIFE

DID YOU KNOW?

Some puffin burrows are over three feet long and can take a whole week to dig!

Whoosh! A puffin swoops down and lands on a rocky cliff.

Puffins live on steep cliffs by the sea. These small birds love cold, windy coasts. They spend most of the year far out on the ocean.

In spring, puffins fly back to land. They dig **burrows** in the grassy cliff tops. A burrow is like a small tunnel in the dirt, just big enough for a puffin family.

The cliffs are busy and loud. Puffins stand in rows along the edges, looking out at the crashing waves below. These rocky homes have everything puffins need.

PUFFIN PLACES

Squawk! A horned puffin calls from its perch in Alaska.

Puffins live in the cold parts of the world. Atlantic puffins are found near Iceland, Norway, and Canada.

Horned puffins live near Alaska and the North Pacific Ocean. Tufted puffins share those same coasts. All three types need cold water full of fish and rocky cliffs near chilly seas for nesting.

You will not find puffins in warm places. They need icy seas where their favorite fish swim. The colder, the better!

POCKET PALS
FUN FACT!
The tufted puffin is the biggest puffin, weighing almost two pounds — twice as heavy as its Atlantic cousin!

Thump! A small puffin lands right on the edge of a tall cliff.

Puffins are small birds. They stand about ten inches tall — that's shorter than a ruler! Next to a seagull, they look tiny.

A puffin weighs about one pound. You could hold one in two hands. Its body is round and chunky, shaped like a little football.

Even though puffins are small, they are tough. They swim through icy waves, fly through strong winds, and dig deep burrows. These little birds are stronger than they look!

BRIGHT BEAKS

A puffin's beak glows under ultraviolet light — scientists just discovered this in 2018!

Click! Two puffins tap their bright orange beaks together.

Puffins are easy to spot. They have black and white feathers like tiny penguins. But their beak is what makes them special. It has bold stripes of orange, red, and yellow.

A puffin's beak gets brighter in spring. This helps them attract a mate. After summer ends, the bright colors fade away until next year.

Puffins also have bright orange feet. Their webbed toes help them paddle through the water with ease. From beak to toe, puffins are built for the sea.

SUPER SIGHT

Puffins can tell their mate apart just by the sound of their call!

Splash! A puffin spots a tiny fish deep under the waves.

Puffins can see very well underwater. They spot fish even in dark, cloudy water. Even more impressive, puffins can see ultraviolet light, which makes certain fish scales glow and easier to track in the deep. Their eyes also adjust focus instantly between air and water, which most animals cannot do.

Each eye has a clear cover that slides shut when they dive. It works like tiny goggles! This keeps their eyes safe in the salty sea.

Puffins also have sharp hearing. They can recognize their mate's call from far away, even in a colony of thousands of noisy birds.

STAY SAFE

Tufted puffins grow long golden feather tufts that sweep back from their heads like fancy hair!

Growl! A puffin puffs up and snaps its beak at a rival.

Puffins have clever ways to stay safe. Their dark backs blend in with the dark ocean below. Their white bellies match the bright sky above. This means predators looking up or down struggle to spot them against the light.

This coloring is called countershading. It works best when puffins float on the open water, making them nearly invisible to hungry gulls above and large fish below.

When enemies get too close anyway, puffins fight back hard. Their strong beaks can bite hard enough to draw blood, and they will not let go easily. Most predators learn their lesson fast!

FISH
FEAST
DID YOU KNOW?
Sand eels are so small that a
hungry puffin might eat over 40
in a single day!
16

Gulp! A puffin swallows a small fish in one big bite.

Puffins love to eat fish. Their favorite is the sand eel, a thin silvery fish that swims in huge schools just below the surface. They also snap up herring, capelin, and whatever else is swimming by.

What makes puffins special is how they catch their food. They dive underwater and actually fly through the water using their wings as flippers, chasing fish at speeds up to 10 miles per hour!

A puffin needs around 40 fish every single day just for itself. Swimming, diving, and flying burns enormous energy. All those fish keep a puffin strong and ready to do it all again tomorrow!

DIVE DEEP

Splash! A puffin folds its wings and dives into the sea.

Puffins hunt by diving deep into the ocean. They use their wings to swim underwater. It looks like they are flying through the sea!

A puffin can hold many fish in its beak at once. Small spines inside its mouth grip each fish tight. This lets it catch more without dropping any.

Puffins can dive down 200 feet — that is deeper than Niagara Falls is tall! They hold their breath and chase schools of fish through the cold, dark water.

One puffin was spotted with 62 tiny fish stuffed into its beak at once — a world record!

WATCH OUT

Skuas are pirate birds that chase puffins in the air and steal fish right out of their beaks!

Screech! A big gull swoops toward a puffin on the cliff.

Puffins face many dangers. Great black-backed gulls are one of their worst enemies. These huge birds patrol the colonies, stealing eggs and snatching young **pufflings** right off the cliff face.

At sea, puffins must watch for large fish and hungry seals lurking below the surface. On land, arctic foxes are clever enough to dig right into burrows to reach eggs and chicks hidden inside.

Living in a large colony is one of their best defenses. Thousands of pairs of eyes watching at once means danger gets spotted fast. One alarm call and the whole colony is on high alert in seconds!

QUICK ESCAPE

Horned puffins nest on rocky ledges so steep that foxes cannot climb up to reach them!

Zoom! A puffin takes off from the water to escape danger.

Puffins have a few ways to escape. On land, they dash into their burrows and hide. Underground, they are safe from gulls and other hungry birds.

In the water, puffins dive fast. They slip below the surface in a flash. Most enemies cannot follow them down into the dark depths.

Puffins can also take off from the water. They flap hard and skip across the waves, then lift up into the sky. Within seconds, they are gone!

FLY FAST

DID YOU KNOW?
Puffins cannot soar or glide like eagles — they must flap nonstop or they will fall!

Whirr! A puffin beats its tiny wings as fast as it can.

Puffins may look clumsy, but they are fast flyers. They beat their wings up to 400 times a minute! That is so fast their wings become a blur.

A puffin can fly up to 55 miles per hour. Their wings are short but powerful. They must work hard every second to stay in the air.

Landing is the tricky part. Puffins sometimes tumble and roll when they touch down. Some even crash right into other puffins on the crowded cliffs!

BUSY BIRDS

26

Squawk! A puffin stretches its wings in the morning sun.

Puffins are busy from morning to night. They fly out to sea to hunt for fish, then come back to rest on the cliffs. They **preen** their feathers in the sunshine.

Puffins spend a lot of time cleaning their feathers. Smooth, clean feathers keep them warm and dry. This is very important for birds that spend so much time in cold water.

At night, puffins tuck into their burrows to sleep. They feel safe in the dark underground, cozy and hidden from danger.

COLONY CREW

FUN FACT!
One puffin colony in Iceland has more than one million birds!

Brawk! Hundreds of puffins call out at once on the cliff.

Puffins live in big groups called colonies. Some colonies have thousands of birds! They all nest on the same cliff or island, packed close together.

Living in a group keeps puffins safer. So many eyes are always watching. It is hard for enemies to sneak up when the whole colony stays alert.

Even in a huge group, puffins know their own mate. Each pair shares one burrow year after year. The whole colony feels like a busy, noisy town.

BILLING BEAKS

Click, click! Two puffins rub their beaks side by side.

Puffins pick one mate and stay together for many years. Each spring, they meet at the same burrow. The two birds greet each other by rubbing beaks together. This sweet hello is called **billing**.

Billing is a way for puffins to show love. Other puffins gather around to watch. It is like a little party on the cliff!

After billing, the pair gets ready to have a baby. They fix up their burrow with soft grass and feathers. Soon it will be warm and cozy for an egg.

PUFFY PUFFLINGS

Crack! A fluffy puffin chick pecks its way out of its egg.

A baby puffin is called a puffling. It hatches from a single white egg deep inside the burrow. The tiny chick is covered in soft, dark, fuzzy down.

Pufflings cannot see well at first. They stay hidden in the warm burrow where it is safe. But the little chick grows fast on a diet of fish.

After about six weeks, the puffling is big enough to leave. It walks out of the burrow at night and heads to the sea all alone. The ocean is now its home.

TEAM WORK

DID YOU KNOW?
Puffin parents may bring back over 1,000 fish for one chick in a single summer!

Flap! A parent puffin brings a beak full of fish to its chick.

Both puffin parents take care of their chick. They take turns sitting on the egg to keep it warm. It takes about 40 days to hatch.

Once the puffling arrives, the real work starts. Both parents fly to sea and bring back fish. They may make ten trips or more each day!

The parents keep feeding the chick for about six weeks. Then they leave, and the puffling must find its own way to the sea. It is ready to start life on its own.

LOSING HOMES

Crash! Big waves pound a puffin's cliff as the storm grows.

Puffins are in trouble. The ocean is warming, pushing their favorite fish into deeper, colder water further offshore. When fish disappear from their usual spots, parent puffins cannot find enough food to keep their chicks alive.

Oil spills and plastic pollution make things worse. Trash floating in the ocean entangles birds and poisons the fish puffins depend on.

Some colonies have lost more than half their birds in just a few decades. But people are fighting hard to protect them!

HELPING HANDS

Click! A scientist puts a tiny tracker on a puffin's leg.

People all over the world are helping puffins. Scientists study where puffins go and what they eat. This helps them learn exactly what puffins need to survive.

In some places, puffins had completely disappeared. But people brought them back! They set out wooden decoy puffins to attract real ones. And it worked!

Kids can help too. Picking up beach trash keeps the ocean safe for puffins and fish. When we care about these colorful birds, we help them grow strong for years to come.

GLOSSARY

burrow

A hole or tunnel dug in the ground where an animal lives.

puffling

A baby puffin.

billing

When two puffins rub their beaks together to bond.

colony

A large group of animals that live together in one place.

preen

To clean and smooth feathers with the beak.